the PARIS I love...

Photography by PATRICE MOLINARD

Introduction by MARCEL AYMÉ

Titles by ANTOINE BLONDIN

Text by JEAN-PAUL CLÉBERT

TUDOR PUBLISHING COMPANY
New York City 3

THERE are some who would have us believe that Parisians do not know their own city. In my view, however, the allegation is too sweeping. It would be nearer the mark to say that the inhabitants are familiar only with such parts of Paris as they need to know in their pursuit of livelihood and recreation; the quarter where they dwell, the one where they work, and of course the boulevards and the Champs-Elysées, where they go to behold such outstanding figures of the age as Lollobrigida and Audrey Hepburn on the screen. Add to these the streets round about the Rue St-Honoré, where may be observed the changing face of fashion; and also a few big stores, some exhibition halls, the Invalides, the Eiffel Tower. Nor should I overlook the great railway terminals, their names evocative of holidays or of war.

As may be seen, this takes in a good

deal of ground. With only so much knowledge at his command, the historian a thousand years hence would readily be able to reconstruct the universe of today's Parisian—barring always a few such exceptions as the Cour de Rohan and the Church of St-Julien-le-Pauvre. A lot of water has gone under the bridges of the Seine since those two historical relics, to name no others, have figured as landmarks in the course of daily life; and it would be unthinkable nowadays if a man, at the close of his week in the shop or office, were to suggest to his family that they treat themselves to a Saturday afternoon at the Sainte-Chapelle. His wife and children would greet any such proposal in no uncertain terms, and he himself—assuming he had set his mind upon this pilgrimage of self-improvement—would carry through with small enthusiasm. All feel alike the common preference for history in the making over history that is past. They would rather have a share, be it ever so modest, in whatever goes on right now. History, for them, is the greening of the grass on the Buttes-Chaumont, or the Franco-Austrian soccer game, or Hitchcock's latest film.

After all, isn't visiting a centuries-old

church or palace like going to call on an old man? Supposing he is remarkably well preserved, that he has a ready wit and a wealth of salty recollections. Even so, his grandnephews will get more of a "boot" out of the latest jive or the salient aspects of Sophia Loren. Not to mention the fact that those storied piles of musty stone give off a learned chill, which is not "cool." A Louis XIII, château or a Roman cloister—junk heaps like those are good enough to poke around in when you're on vacation and you have a rainy day to kill. But not here. They just aren't in the groove.

Such indifference on the part of Parisians toward the cherished things of old need not in itself cause any sense of outrage. At the Sainte-Chapelle, one has to admit, "audience participation" is ever so much more limited than at the Vel d'Hiv or the Gaumont Palace. Nor is it in the least extraordinary that people should pass by the Louvre and St-Germain-l'Auxerrois without ever seeing them. Standing aside, as those venerable buildings do, from the paths of the daily grind, they are gratifying objects for the curiosity of sightseers from abroad.

Perhaps the outstanding merit of this

album is that it brings so many of those esteemed monuments back into the very forefront of the present day. Let anyone who has eyes, whether he be a Parisian or not, leaf through these pages more than once (as he will wish to do), and he can not help but learn that a history-laden façade is no mere entity, separate and apart, drawn in upon the aloofness of its own past: that it has, instead, become somehow all involved and mixed up with the sky, or maybe with a tree, or with the periwinkle blue of a flower girl's eyes or the skeleton of the Eiffel Tower or the shopfront of a creamery, or with a veil of mist, or a calf's head poking out of a housewife's market bas-ket... or with whatever arrangement of things in the bloom of life one's mood or fancy dictates, wheresoever one may please. Certain of these pictures plainly show that any structure at all, no matter how hoary with age, may be imaged in the retrospect of some Parisian's head and heart.

In and out among the photographs by Patrice Molinard there runs the tumb-ling brook of Antoine Blondin's text. To make the stones of Paris come alive and sing, no better man could have been found than this Villonesque young poet-novelist; and were I not cramped for space, I should at this point like nothing better than to relate the strange tale of Blondin's life. For that would be, amid the roses and raptures, to go right on writing about Paris all day, all night, and so into the dawn.

To supplement these pictures and set them in their proper frame, we have also the illuminating commentary of Jean-Paul Clébert, whose presentation bears witness both to his knowledge of the city and his understanding of its human values.

When you have read the notes and commentary by Clébert and Blondin, and have scanned the pictures from cover to cover you might care to play a harmless little game, and one which has a not-too-remote bearing upon the world of things as they are. Here's how it goes. If Paris were to be caught in the atomic crossfire of world fury, and if only a single monument (or a street or a quarter) were by some miracle to escape destruction, which would you choose to have it be...? It is an amusing game which can be played as solitaire if you wish, but any number can play and it is of course more fun in company.

MARCEL AYMÉ.

The heart of Paris is a stony heart where Notre-Dame lies stranded, like a heavy-laden barque of masonry, against the Right Bank of the Seine. Here is the favorite rendez-vous of young lovers, who clamber boldly about among the upper-works to plot the course of more remote excursions, to trace the outline of the older town within the spreading city — to take a bird's eye view of life itself, and of the distant future. How easy it is to cry out "Lift up your heart!" when your head is 200 feet up in the air and you are in love! In Paris, though, a match that's made in heaven by no means always rings the wedding bell.

At first sight, like the fleeting glimpse of some pretty girl in a train window, Paris can make you catch your breath. But it may also happen that your feeling at the outset is one of disappointment, for to *love* Paris takes patience... Suppose, let us say, that you are coming in from New York and you set foot in the Gare Saint-Lazare for the first time. If the weather in the streets be only the least bit grey, tinged with that pearly softness of the Ile-de-France which is too evanescent to leap at once to the eye, you will experience a letdown. The houses are tall and black and streaked with soot. They are un-dignified piles of late nineteenth-century non-descript. Every street-crossing is blocked with motor cars which distract attention and impede the view. To escape from this dingy matrix of dust and grime in which Parisians are coated, as it were with a second skin, up to their chins, you should take to your heels down the Rue Pasquier and plunge like a swimmer into the leafy green of the Square Louis XVI. There you can catch your breath and start to find your bearings. The new-comer, though, is not always aware of this refuge. Nor will shame permit me to dwell upon those other approaches into Paris, whether by way of the Gare d'Austerlitz, de Lyon, du Nord, de l'Est, at

a snail's pace through grimy slums — New York, Tokyo, and Berlin can teach us nothing in this respect — where the traveler is condemned to linger in canyons rough-hewn through buildings that have been chopped apart by main force, their windows gaping like open wounds... No, Paris does not put forward her best foot to greet the new arrival.

However, to appreciate the great city, one need not be a Parisian born, nor even live here. Many foreigners and more Frenchmen from the provinces come here only in summer, perhaps for a month or two in the year; yet often they know more about Paris than Parisians do. They visit the city with a thoroughness which merits our respect. Thus it is that some of the natives of Monterey (California) or La Ciotat (Bouches-du-Rhône) have an understanding of the capital comparing favorably with ours. Such travelers — I use the word in preference to "tourists", which carries something of a slur — have a power which we have lost. They have the "innocent eye", the unjaded viewpoint, and need only rid themselves, as they quickly do, of preconceptions based on souvenir post-cards and documentary films. We, on the other hand, are too close to the subject and can no longer see what stares us in the face the whole day long. Their eye for the unusual is quicker than our own, and we are wonderstruck at what they find to wonder at.

This past year, interviewing a large number of foreigners newly arrived from every corner of the globe, I have asked what it was that struck them first of all. A woman from Brazil was astounded

Crossing your bridges as you come to them, you may hopefully seek out a room with a view across the rooftops. Those who have no roofs, bed down beneath the bridges ; but the reverse of the proposition is not true. As a usual thing, your Parisian is oblivious to the sea of zinc and slate and tile that billows over his town — whether because he has too much on his mind or is in too deep a rut, I cannot say. Nor does he really start worrying until the very day when he finds himself once more with the lease run out. Then it is that in his mind's eye, prying beneath this jumble of crazy box lids, he sees all the good little tenants tidily tucked away in their apartments, lined up like so many toy soldiers in their appointed slots. Wherefore, possibly, we have come to speak of finding one's niche in life... Be that as it may, there stands the Palais de Justice to bring his roving fancy down to earth, while the spire of the Sainte-Chapelle is a pointed reminder that fairer mansions are to be found on high.

The Abbey of St-Germain-des-Prés completed in the 12th Century, looked down in former times upon the meadow called the Pré aux Clercs, where duels were fought, and where the Fair of St-Germain used to be held. There sprigs of the nobility, on the lookout for the fairest of the Fair, would come to mingle with the students. The fight continues to this very day, except that now it is a struggle for tables at the three literary cafés where midnight is merely the shank of the evening. As for the fair, it still enjoys a sort of marginal existence — on the cuff, as it were — for here we may see the French quietly getting back a little of their own by needling the young tourist who has to sing for his supper. This is only tit for tat, since it is here that eager trippers have long flocked from overseas to observe the flaming youth of France at its most torrid. For many years the warm regard was mutual but there is a hint of frost beneath the awnings nowadays.

at the concierges. "Strange characters", was what she found them, "living in funny dens", their walls papered with pages torn out of old house-furnishing catalogues; and they put her in mind, she said, of the *tricoteuses* of French Revolutionary times who went out into the streets to harangue the mob and take blood vengeance on victims of their private grudges. To this very day, said she, they wield their brooms like weapons and passers-by are plainly fearful of them.

The horse-meat butchers, too, had caught this fair Brazilian's attention: could you conceive of anything more revolting? And with a sign out front in the form of a horse's head! Why, outside the horse market in the Rue Brancion, they have even carried this cruelty to animals to the point of putting up a memorial bust of M. Émile Decroix, who sold the French people the idea of eating horse meat. And as for the cafés! You see them everywhere you look. Parisians give the impression of spending their whole time there. Are these all the homes they have? Women can go to cafés unescorted and the waiters are accomodating. You can trust them with a suitcase. One in particular had astonished the lady from Rio: he doubled as waiter and actor. When he was through serving, he quit the counter to go and cut a caper in the theater next door. Right in front of the patrons he put on a long overcoat and long-toed shoes and a comical hat, took up a walking stick, and assumed the expression of a mournful clown. Only in Paris could you see such a thing.

The *Quai des Célestins*, in one of its good moods, presents the very image of that leisurely release from care which this miraculously unspoiled metropolis can still provide, thus drawing to itself, despite the deflation of the myth of " Gay Paree ", the hopeful foreigner in his search for sheer delight. Later this evening, in this very spot, a rosy-fingered twilight will rise up from the river to blend with the answering sky; the tugboat, towing night along at the end of its quivering cable, will head downriver toward the sea, and the passerby will discover that Paris la nuit *can mean more than one thing.*

A man from Brazil (it merely so happened; he might as well have been a Mexican or a Ukrainian) told me about his first night in Paris. He had registered at a flea bag in the Rue de la Grande-Chaumière for the simple reason that that name had long been running through his head. The room was small and dark. The main article of furniture was a bed like an iron cage, such as he had seen in surrealist movies, and the bolster gave him a momentary shock. He turned in but found that he was too excited to go to sleep.

The idea of *being in Paris* obsessed him. So up he got, to look out in the street and view the City of Light. But the window opened upon — nothing. He went and threw open the door, telling himself that the first person he encountered was bound to be someone fabulous. In the corridor there was not a soul. Going in search of a window, all he could find was a tiny airhole in a broom closet. And even then he had to stand on a chair in order to see out. But the peephole opened only on to an inner courtyard, grimy and steep as a mine shaft. He craned his neck — and just at that moment the proprietress stepped out of doors and saw him.

"What are you looking for?" she shouted. "If it's Jeannette you're after, she's gone."

The Brazilian withdrew in confusion.

Thus it is that Paris gradually reveals itself; in short takes, so to say, one step at a time. And on foot is precisely how you should learn your way about, as if exploring a jungle. Parisian life is not

The old quarters of this city do not wear the aspect of those museum pieces which are to be found in some capitals. Nothing slumbrous clings to the flanks of Notre-Dame — nothing meekly resigned to snuggle beneath the touched-up shroud of artifice. Contrary to what this prospect might suggest, the bridges linking the history of Paris with everyday life are never down. Hemmed in though it is on every side by the remembrance of things past, the Ile de la Cité keeps up its contact with the world; and few indeed are the dwellers upon either bank who do not find time to spare a daily glance at their old cathedral, where it stands as a reminder that Paris is well worth a Mass.

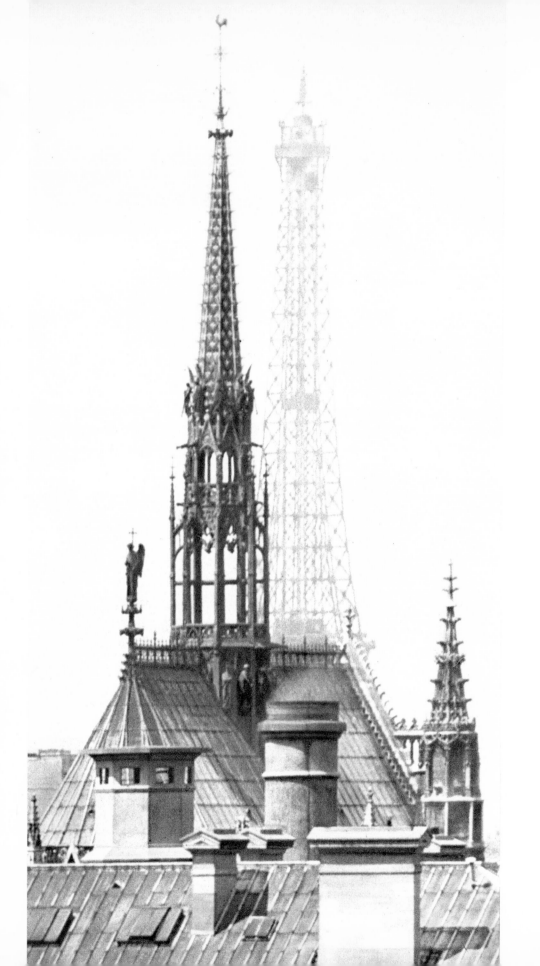

The skyline of Paris is a populous one. There, inscribed on an azure field, is the precious lineage that links the twentieth-century city and the ancient Cité — the happy inter-marriage of weathered stone and modern steel, bound not so much by common mortar as by the firm cement of time. To the left, that metallic giraffe which is about to leap upon the spindly stork is the Eiffel Tower, crowding up against the spire of the Sainte-Chapelle. The tricky eye of the telephoto lens has brought them thus together — but what matter if this is only an optical illusion? It is as nothing beside the composition of unrelated objects, brought together by an inscrutable Providence, which appears above. One could ask for no better allegorical representation of Progress going hand in hand with Tradition. For we are in the midst of the Quartier St-Antoine, the cradle of revolution and the stamping ground of riot. Yet it would appear that the equilibristic Spirit of the Bastille, the ageless emblem of freedom forever won, would like nothing better than to wing his way elsewhere. So beguiling is the tender air of Paris that no doubt he would have hopped off long ago, if only he could decide which of the two bell towers to perch upon.

to be found only in the great buildings. You may track it also across the sandstone pavements, among the weeds, in the hoary buildings of the town, which have the air of wayside inns left over from days of old. You will find it on the plane surfaces of the city's dilapidated walls, rich in those values which today's photographers and abstract painters seek, whereon the kids have scrawled their immemorial *graffiti* — bleeding hearts transfixed with arrows, death's heads adorned with incidental hair — and artless expressions of affection (*I love Lili the belle of Javel*) and of mystification (*The worm will turn! Across the street they sell crutches for centipedes*). And you may see it in the hop-scotch patterns of the very young, who chalk horizontal totem poles along the sidewalks, adorned with numerals or with symbols ranging down from Heaven to Hell.

The life that is Paris takes form in the branching posts of the ancient gaslights, with their resemblance to the gallows. And it abides in the wicker and rattan chairs where the concierges plump themselves down outside their doors, to pursue their needlework and exchange their endless gossip.

To visit Paris, one must accomodate oneself to the hour, the day, and the weather. The Halles are at their best at three in the morning beneath a fine spring rain. The Place du Tertre is best seen in a late-winter twilight when serrated roofs and the bare branches of the plane trees stand clear against the cold. The end of a summer's afternoon is the right time for the quays of the Seine, with the sun,

The fisherman is a paralytic by choice. The great buildings that gaze blankly out across the Quai Conti are not more immobile. What does he catch? He catches cold. No need to remind him that Paris once was called Lutetia — he knew her when. And that is why, day in day out, he stands there while the cork at the end of his line obeys the motto of the city's heraldic ship: Fluctuat nec Mergitur. It tosses but it never sinks.

As with every monument, Notre-Dame may be put to use in various ways. You can photograph it from above or paint it from below. Down in the square you are exposed to the nuisance of playing to the crowd but up on the balcony you can overlook the hubbub and play gargoyle. Here the American sharpshooter turns his back on the ossified birds (restored) which are chimaeras, dear to the heart of Quasimodo. Today it would seem as if their noses are out of joint on account of the blonde competition. But the soldier, intent upon the lure of the antique, will accept no substitutes.

red as a child's balloon, slowly sinking behind the Ile de la Cité. Mid-January, in the coldest season of the year, is best for the neighborhood of the Porte des Lilas, when the icy gale sweeps the ridges bare and stark, transforming them to the semblance of the Siberian tundra.

As for the Champs-Elysées, the time is ten o'clock of a June morning, for then the young girls in all their splendor seem as though they had sprung into blossom overnight.

The street names of Paris are something special, too. Regrettable though it is that nowadays the streets are called, more often than not, in honor of the estimable unknown, the names do sometime shave a touch of the fresh and unexpected — *Gracieuse*, *Tournefort*, *Monsieur*, *Princesse*, *de Pélican*, *des Cinq-Diamants*, *Brisemiche* — or Broken Bread. And God alone would seem to rate the designation of two thoroughfares: the *Passage Dieu* between the Rues des Haies and des Orteaux, in Ménilmontant, and the *Rue Dieu* on the Quai de Valmy. But the first Dieu was only a landlord on the erstwhile alley and the second a general who fell at Solferino... Occasionally, too, we find a street with its name twisted by popular usage, the dwellers along it having baptized it anew to suit their taste. That is why the *Rue de la Reynie*, in the Halles, is invariably pronounced *Rue de l' Araignée* — Spider Street. It even sounds prettier that way! Which reminds me of a friend who set out to find the *Rue Guillaume Apollinaire*. Through the dark he wandered to and fro where it ought to

To see this laden barge nosing its way upriver, one might suppose the Seine a hospitable stream. For centuries, though, the kings jealously protected Parisian boatmen's rights by compelling outsiders who used the port to share the returns on their cargoes with the natives. Fifty-fifty was the rule of the house; and a thousand years ran underneath the bridges before a freighter such as this could get by without paying toll to the local water rats.

be, until finally he gave up and went to the police station. The desk sergeant admitted he never had heard of it. Out came the official guidebook. No sign of Apollinaire. They looked under Guillaume. Not there. But my friend knew for certain that there was such a street. Back and forth through the book they leafed and checked, but all in vain. At last my friend, elbowing the cop aside to get a better look, chanced upon the entry G. Apollin, the abbreviation to which the tight columns of the guidebook had cut it down. "There", he pointed uncertainly. "Oh," said the cop, "*Rue Gapollin!* Why couldn't you say so in the first place?"

One of the street names that pleases me best is *Panoyaux*, which leaves a fine fruity flavor on the tongue.

As a matter of taste, also, it seems to me a pity that impersonal numbers have been substituted for the oldtime names of the various quarters of the town. Fortunately, police commissariats preserve those robust old designations on their façades. Who would not rather live in *le Gros-Caillou* than the Seventh Arrondissement? In *Les Grandes-Carrières* and *la Goutte-d'Or* than the Eighteenth? Or in *la Folie-Méricourt* than the Eleventh?

Moving on to questions of a different sort of taste, we come naturally to places of refreshment. Here, I can do no better than treat you to some of the vintage names, such as *Quatre Sergents de la Rochelle, Enfants Terribles, la Closerie des Lilas, Café des Phares, Trois Rats, Rendez-vous des Douaniers, la*

Looking across from the balcony of th Louvre, we are confronted by a view of the Institut. There assembles th Académie Française, thus qualifying tha structure too as a museum. Since th means of transit is designated simpl Footbridge of the Arts, pedestrians migh easily become confused between the two Not so the members of the Académie They have had their eyes fixed on the dom of the Institut from afar, intent upon mak ing their way to a seat beneath it. This i easier said than done. The ascent i tricky and the scholar, like the stroller must watch his step, for the slopes o Parnassus are strewn with stumbling blocks. However, once onstalled as Aca démiciens, they take a new lease on life and when they venture to sally forth, it ma be observed that although there are season when the trees are bare, the Immortals ar always in full fig.

The Tour St-Jacques, here seemingly caught in the act of adjusting a feather boa, is a very old lady indeed. Standing all alone in the midst of a tiny garden, it might readily be taken for an architectural freak of the Châtelet. But that would be too flippant a dismissal of the fact that once upon a time it served as guidepost for pilgrims on the way to Compostella and as a watchtower against the approach of invaders. Nowadays, when people are more likely to go on junkets than pilgrimages, invasion not only is welcomed but invited. Transient guest or honorary citizen, it makes no difference — all may enjoy the freedom of the city; and so, like Rastignac, we find there are a thousand ways of laying siege to Paris. Take the country cousin on our left, who has checked his sabots in the suburbs and bought himself a new suit in which to pay his respects to the Eiffel Tower; or the duet of Dutch Eagle Scouts getting in the groove at the river's brink. A squint through the telescope on the terrace of the Sacré-Cœur is a good way to spy out the ground.

Promenade de Vénus, la Clé des Champs, Bouquet des Dames, Sanglier qui Fume, and latlys the *Café de la Banquise* (crowded in summer, less so in winter), which signifies "iceberg".

Photography, as in this album, is an indispensable adjunct to our search. It sharpens our power of vision, so to speak, as if with a third eye. For the camera's eye includes and makes us see what we never could learn to envision for ourselves: a chance effect of lighting, the instantaneous perception that eludes our sight, the human figure caught precisely right within the frame, and, timed to the fraction of a second in some place where we were not, a gesture held in mid-motion, a burst of sunshine and the play of light and shade... And this heightening of perception we owe to the telephoto lens. For thus we are enabled to take in the Place de la Concorde and the Obelisk at a single glance, together with the Quartier Saint-Lazare and the Butte des Moulins, four landscapes all in one, since, from the banks of the Seine, we are looking clear to the northernmost horizon of the city. It is a revelation. In less than the twinkling of an eye, Paris stands transformed according to the perspectives of Fra Angelico. "Teleobjectivity" restores to us the visual technique of the Italian Primitives.

Let no one say that this is false perspective simply because it is not that of the human eye. Who knows but what it faithfully renders the purview of pigeons, or of the statues atop the Chamber of Deputies... ?

Symbol of former conquests : the charioteer atop the Grand Palais. A prisoner of history, left at the post in spite of his many laurels, he is going nowhere fast. Perhaps, being only bronze, he does not care, and yet... is he not saluting the mammiferous contours of the Sacré-Cœur with a despairing gesture ? This charioteer is precisely what the young man on the preceding page is viewing through the glass.

Enveloped between the sweeping pincers of the Louvre, the Arc de Triomphe du Carrousel signalizes Napoleon's victories. More reminiscent, at this season, of the Retreat from Moscow is the fugitive figure in the fur coat, for whom the gate to the Tuileries stands open; but the man has still to make good his passage of the Berezina — the Place de la Concorde, a crossing, as we know, not entirely without its perils.

Above all, Paris is no mere out-of-door museum piece, no dead city to be inspected in silence like the ruins of Pompei. It is no open-air Louvre on a yet grander scale, its stones glossed over with the patina of age and frozen into the context of their historical significance. Paris, teeming like a drop of water beneath the lens of the microscope, is a city which throbs with the vigor of pulsing life. It is forever in the act of giving birth — a monstrous and prolific cannibal, devouring and digesting even its own bricks. The thousand years of Notre-Dame by no means summarize its story, nor the 291 steps of the Tour Saint-Jacques. Paris also means the morning subway ride, so bitterly complained of... the cause of so much grumbling that if you but show the French in Caracas a canceled métro ticket, you will wring their hearts.

If you would understand Paris, you must know its personal histories, the miscellaneous news items in its dailies, the last of its wooden paving blocks, its passions and its crimes. You ought to know (I am choosing at random from the first copy of *Paris-Soir* that comes to hand) what happened today at 28, Rue des Favorites. It says here that a man blew up the penthouse at that address in an attempt to commit suicide by gas. And here it says that a parakeet has tied up traffic for an hour in the Rue Saint-Dominique. Seems the bird escaped from a garret window and went footing it solemnly along the right of way until the firemen had to be called to try to catch it. Paris...

As a rule, churches are somber and houses bright. Looking up from the foot of Montmartre, we see the reverse. At night, however, the mystery is explained when these houses spring to life in an eerie neon glare which turns the Barbès-Rochechouart intersection into a sort of frontier post between Pigalle and La Chapelle ; a district within a ward where the extremes of toil and pleasure meet. Streets here would be more than a little uninviting after dark were it not for the protective bulk of the Basilica, that Annapurna where it is always Sunday afternoon, presiding over all.

Item : you might like to know that the super-intendent of the dog cemetery, Pont de Clichy, is M. Alexandre Dumas, and that Jean Cocteau, it says here, is a painting contractor.

There is, however, still another Paris, which comes as a delightful surprise. Beneath the over-passes of the métro and along the esplanades and on the bowling greens of Ménilmontant taverns, they play *pétanque*, which is the Italian *ballo*, with the rules of the game improvised as it goes along. On the Quai de la Tournelle, a certified professor teaches spear fishing. Fat oxen still are driven through the Rue de Crimée. There is a war on flying cockroaches; people go out at dawn to pick mushrooms under the sycamores; and by night they glimpse the silent passage of the river barges.

Paris is a port of dreams. From its quays are launched strange voyages and in the labyrinth of its eighty-five hundred streets (744 miles) you lose your way but find a thousand marvels.

Just for fun, let us sketch the life history of a self-made Parisian; by which I mean, of course, that he brings himself up in the direction he wants to go. As his years unfold, he will apply himself to the exacting art of getting the most of what his city has to offer. His place of birth should be in the Cité, somewhere between the fringe of trees that screens the riverside and the stone buttresses of Notre-Dame. He will learn his rudiments in the Latin Quarter and spin his top in the side streets off the Boul'Mich; his adolescence, a bit studious, a bit inquisitive but devoted to loafing,

The Place du Tertre, if not precisely the top of the world, is the high point of a microcosm, Montmartre. Those hardy mountaineers, the landscape painters, who scale its sides with their easels at all seasons of the year, have worked it over with the hues of a rich palette, and rightly so. But you may view it at its most appealing on some wintry morning such as this, when there is a nip in the air and everything is muted with snowy white. Come summer, though, when Montmartre, breaking out in a rash of striped umbrellas, is crawling with Cadillac convertibles and glad rags, those who love the place no longer can see it for dust.

The Conciergerie skulks behind the Palais de Justice but it looms larger when one takes the longer view. Time was when these twin towers deserved the inscription Dante saw above the gates of Hell, for between them passed the condemned victims of the Reign of Terror, there to kill the hours until their summons to the scaffold. Years have lent the old prison a mellower aspect. When April is in the wind, springtime contrives to soften the scene with a frame of tender foliage, more in keeping with the prospects of the young girl who lives across the moat. She has no time to kill except the hours between dances as she flings to the breeze a banner fresh-dipped in couleur de rose.

mostly, will be spent in Saint-Germain-des-Prés, where also he will fall in love; and after that he will discover the pleasures of the arts on Montparnasse. But then the day will come — supposing he lacks the divine fire and, realizing it, resolves to face up to the duller things of life — when he must cross the river to gain experience and settle down to work. He earns a livelihood around the Halles, or gravitates toward the Bourse, sets up housekeeping in the Marais, and opens an office on the Champs-Elysées. Glory and renown beckon him toward the Invalides or the Quai d'Orsay. He grows portly, however, on Montmartre, seeks out a quiet retreat in the Paris hinterland, which is to say Auteuil or Ménilmontant, and discreetly goes to rest in Père-Lachaise, which is every right-thinking Parisian's place of last repose...

As one crosses over the Ile de la Cité, which was the cradle of Paris, the notion strikes one that when Moses went adrift in his cradle, he was hardly less secure than were the first Lutetians who here found refuge among the bulrushes in midstream. Yet, from that lowly sandbar have arisen the beetling cliffs of the Prefecture of Police and the towering trunk of the Sainte-Chapelle and the huge frame of Notre-Dame, where it stands with all its ribs exposed and looking, from certain angles, like a dinosaur in the midst of a deserted museum. For it is true that, except for a few shreds clinging to the apse of the cathedral, the living flesh that once was Paris has here been sloughed off. (Yes, and the Rues Chanoinesse and des Ursins, de la

This stricken athlete is one of the masterpieces in the open-air museum devoted to the work of Rodin, admirable but a trifle melancholy, in the courtyard of the Hôtel Biron. It represents the dying Adam, in those days when the idea of death was as yet unknown — when the primal instance of the "last slumber" seemed like a drowsiness descending upon the frame of Nature itself.

 the right, the dome of the
 Invalides ; to the left, the
 héon — thus preserving the
t distinction. The former
rs the remains of Napoleon,
or and great soldier. In the
lie Émile Zola and others of
group, famed spokesmen of
cracy who were civilians to the
  To all outward seeming, we
on the one hand a fit setting for
 funerals, on the other a path
 leads but to the grave. They
 by day majestically aloof.
hen the beams of sunset kindle
domes to rosy fire, they become
r of glowing censers distilling
lf-same incense, which to the
ls of ambition is the breath
ory.

Colombe and des Chantres, stand as they did of old).
Otherwise, it is as though this former grumbling
hive of masonry, this erstwhile ant heap of culs-de-
sac and crooked alleys, were subsiding. The Cité
reached its peak of development in the middle of
the last century. Since then the island itself has
been scoured as if with an iron broom, just as was
done a century earlier to its approaches when its
maze of mooring cables was swept away, and also
its nine bridges, swarming with rat's nests and
human habitations.

At the farther end, framed 19th-century style
in leaves and flowers, the Conciergerie sports white
curtains at its windows nowadays. It speaks well
for the concierge. And the squat tower on the
right still bears the name Tour Bon-Bec (i.e.,
"Good Cheer") because the turnkeys have always
been famed for their ready tongues. *"Il n'est bon
bec que de Paris,"* as François Villon put it, long
ago; but he was careful to shun the grim hospital-
ity of these premises.

Upstream, we come to the Ile Saint-Louis,
which the Cité drags along like a barge in tow.
Let us skip the fact that here is an even greater
burden of past significance, with every house
number famous — or infamous — in days of yore.
For here are the poplars which are menaced with
destruction; the city council proposes to cut them
down. If the trees must go, their sole offence will
have been that they put up mushrooms through
the iron grillwork at their feet — or "leather
tongues", as these morels are known locally.

*The Hôtel des Invalides houses not
only dead soldiers but disabled ones,
and some few who are very lively indeed.
The latter are the members of the General
Staff. As we reflect upon this felicitous
arrangement, whereby the victims of war-
fare and those who direct it are gathered
together under the same roof, should we
not feel a stronger conviction that the
Army is a great band of brothers — that
this establishment is in effect a family
hotel? When the Governor-General of
Paris throws open his windows upon the
huge esplanade, he can lord it over everything in sight—except, of course, the bateau
mouche with its load of sightseers,
busily nosing its way under the thirty-two
bridges of Paris and trailing the white
thread of its wake across the foreground
of this supercolossal Louis XIV production, directed by Mansart.*

On the Left Bank, at the far end of the Pont-Saint-Michel, we come to the oldest Paris of all, and the richest in associations. Neither the Boulevard Saint-Germain nor the Rue des Ecoles serve really to give access to this highly fertile hill, which always is spoken of as the Mountain. To traverse it on foot is the one truly Parisian way of journeying into the past. If you would go back through time two hundred or even three hundred years, you need only ascend the Rue de la Montagne-Sainte-Geneviève and thread your way along the Rues de la Huchette and de la Bûcherie until you come to the rabbit warren of Maubert. So little has been changed in these parts that no effort of the imagination is required. The crumbling and weathered stones fairly reek of days gone by.

The Rue Saint-Jacques, skirting this district to the west, is the oldest thoroughfare in our whole city. Ages before Lutetia was founded or human beings came upon the scene, the hairy mammoth trod this pathway, going down to water in the Seine.

In these lower depths of Paris (chronologically speaking) there lingers, like some gas that is heavier than air, the smell of witchcraft. Down blind alleys, behind the closed doors of gloomy vaults, a flourishing business in spells and magic still goes on here. The place is teeming, so they say, with bicentenarians and talking cats and women who have the evil eye. And it is a fact that many a concierge in this quarter does faith-healing. Doctors find poor pickings in Maubert, with their practices cut into by gypsy women and Armenians,

The spell of the great city is exerted not only by its monuments and landmarks. You may feel the same witchery at the foot of some commonplace street when a sudden impression sweeps over you that here runs the nervous system of the world. Perhaps it may be felt as a certain tingling in the air between the sleek walls of the Rue de la Paix, a light-hearted nonchalance which takes hold of the passerby and keys him up to the pitch of Parisian life; or in that organ tone, that note like distant thunder, rumbling among the steep cliffs of the Place de l'Opéra; or maybe it is kindled by the streaming glow of the lighted street signs, forever running away and forever renewed, proclaiming — or so it would seem — that here the weightiest business is transacted in a spirit of carnival. But what really turns the trick is the growing assurance, which increases the further you may go, that Age with his creeping steps can never catch up with the high heels of Paris.

The Opéra, in façade and from the wings. Viewed from outside, the Opéra is a stout and prosperous gentleman, making his weight felt in the city, who conceals a heart of flint beneath the broad expanse of his flashy waistcoat. From behind the scenes it is a covey of little pigeons, served up on a lordly dish — the widest and deepest opera stage of any in the world. The flooring is plank but the discipline is iron.

F*rom the top of the Vendôme Column, Napoleon and a century of catering to the carriage trade look down upon you: " Well done, bright lights of Paris, with which we are well pleased... ! " So let us not feel too surprised if strollers in Paris, for whom more historic vistas unfold than are to be found anywhere else on earth, take all this in their stride. Nor if they flock the streets to go window-shopping by gaslight. Nor if the local talent of St-Germain see fit to stage an impromptu costume ball in the Place Furstenberg. Nor even if, far into the small hours, there is something afoot on the balcony of one of the* grands couturiers.

and by witches left over from a former age who never show themselves by the light of day. For instance, a lingering curse hovers over the Rue Xavier-Privas where all the dwellers in a certain tenement go blind. The latest victim, only last year, was barely able to get out alive.

Between the Rue Galande and the Square Viviani stands one of the oldest churches in Paris, and possibly the most appealing, Saint-Julien-le-Pauvre. Looking as though it were incubating upon a nest of ancient stones, it blends to perfection with the Musée des Trois-Maillets and the saw-toothed gable ends which line the entire street. Nor is it hard to surmise that in the Paris of the future, master-minded by some Le Corbusier of days to come, this tiny enclave of the past will need a fencing of barbed wire and a vigilance committee to preserve it.

Higher up, the atmosphere becomes a little spicy. We have there the "floating population," so called, which ekes out its existence amid a huddle of Chinese grocery stores and working-class cookshops.

Once over the rim, we find that the air is fresher. Paris, it would seem, is in the path of a southerly wind, which is none too cool as it comes blowing up across the Gobelins and the length of the Bièvre until, in the corridor of the Rue Mouffetard, it really heats up. On the far side, the Rue Mouffetard bears more resemblance to a torrent, down which the overflow of Parisian life tumultuously pours. With its grocer's stalls arching out

A spot for meditation where, if you but lift your hand, the air is loud with the wings of greedy pigeons: the Place de l'Étoile, from which twelve avenues diverge. In the midst lies entombed the Unknown Soldier, sheltered within the four porticoes of a massive triumphal arch 147 feet high. The squat pillars of this monument are adorned with bas-reliefs devoted to the celebration of the nation's victories; a strident " Marseillaise " being the most famous panel, by a sculptor with the appropriate name of Rude. Truth to tell, whatever of dignity inheres in the Arc de Triomphe all fires down to the point where burns a perpetual flame which was kindled beneath the vault on November 11, 1920. There it flickers and blows as a reminder to passers-by that not only pigeons ought to flock the scene in hopes of picking up a little grain... of common sense.

This tro[p]
tation
ment of the p
the Church o[f]
deleine, who[se]
rear themselv[es]
cisely the fo[r]
nation lend[s]
baobabs of
can rain fo[r]
bad luck wo[n]
M. le Curé
ping out at t[he]
ment when
shioners are
way in.   N
ter remains
two ladies
stroll throu[gh]
rified jungle
by the simp[le]
putting sca
their heads,
themselves
nave where,
fail, they wi[ll]
they have cr
of those we
all-hours wh
specialty of
Parisian te[mple]
draw to its
many beggar[s]
brities.

dress the bal-
e, the lofty
the pines at
of the Bois
gne suggest
ted shadows
edral. It is
dral which
isk of becom-
lfed in the
f the reflect-
beyond. In
e of history,
enemy squad-
ed out their
o graze here,
y this grove
the meeting
a few well-
t horseback
r whom the
term is
ss.

over the heads of the passers-by, this teeming lower-class thoroughfare puts one in mind of an Arabian fair; and feeding inexhaustibly into it run some of the most picturesque alleyways of the capital: *Rue de l'Arbalète*, *Passage des Patriarches*, *Rue de l'Epée-de-Bois*, *Rue du Pot-de-Fer* and *Rue Ortolan*, which are names to stir the imagination. The Rue Ortolan, however, owes its designation not to the celebrated bird but to an obscure member of the bar whose first name was Elzéar.

From here on stretch the Gobelins, which are, so to say, the true stony jungles of the town. They form a quarter more likely to exhaust the sightseer than he them, since the right way to view them is by shuttling back and forth, turning frequently to retrace one's steps. Every street deserves to be traversed in both directions for the perspective changes entirely when taken the other way. The château de la Reine-Blanche, in the old Ile des Singes, affords as fair a prospect as you will find all in the city. Before finally turning back, make yet one effort more and go to see the Buttes-aux-Cailles and the village of Palmyre, where people speak to one another — their economic interests are interdependent — but regard the denizens of neighboring Denfert with curiosity and suspicion.

At the Luxembourg, where Marie de'Medici's elm trees still are flourishing, Senators, however, have been displaced by baby sitters. But the Gardens preserve a whiff of the very atmosphere Watteau once breathed, the trees he painted, and the bosky shade he loved. If nowadays the scene

When the Grand Duke's away, the mice do play — or, as Parisians call them, les petits rats. *Time was when a score of royal princes passed familiarly beneath the gilded ceilings of the Opéra. These chandeliers have lent their sparkle to commanders, grand cross, of every order of chivalry the world can boast. These mirrors (23 by 33 feet) have reflected the gleaming contours of steel breast-plates and soft bosoms, the silken sashes of the Legion of Honor and of habits which by no means make the monk. Then one by one the gleaming sparks went out. Subscription lists for the Opéra's fêtes galantes, like everything else, have gone off the gold standard, but still the giltwork of the lobbies warmly glows.*

is given over to playing ball and applauding Punch and Judy, still, one ought not to overlook the sixty famous personages who adorn it, elegantly portrayed in stone and ranging all the way from the Comtesse de Ségur to Marius amid the ruins of Carthage.

Beginning at the Place Saint-André-des-Arts and so through to the Moulin-de-Beurre, one finds the teen-agers of Paris, disorderly and passionate, clamorous and amorous. In other words, Saint-Germain-des-Prés and Montparnasse are given over to them. If these two quarters claim today a monopoly of literary glory and the graphic arts, to say nothing of philosophy and psychoanalysis, even so, the brightest jewels in their crown long antedated the touted rise of Existentialism — the only system of thought which has contributed as much to fashions in dress and to myths about Paris as it has to the comprehension of mankind. Grandiose ideas and revolutionary painters and penniless romances have exploded and swirled and eddied about the belfry tower of the Abbaye this many a long year. Before Sartre made the Café Flore his hangout, here was the stamping ground of Charles Maurras and Jean Moréas. And in an epoch even more remote, when the Boulevard Saint-Germain was nothing more than a lower middle-class sidestreet called the Rue Taranne, the intellectual ferment was already seething here. At the start of the 19th century, from the corner of the Rue Gozlin down the length of the Rue des Ciseaux, a structure was erected which was dubbed

In Paris, one learns to distinguish between the banksides that are for sleeping and the quays where people stroll. To saunter by the riverside is a ritual in which townsfolk and tourists engage on an equal footing, all sharing alike, to some degree in the Prodigal Son's emotions upon his return home. For at every moment there is something different to claim the eye; yet everything — from bookstalls to vagabonds, from fishermen to passing barges, from fishline to shoreline — forever is the same.

the Childebert, as the street then was called; and in it congregated a whole shabby-genteel Bohemia whose names today stud the lists of prize volumes awarded in the schools. In due course their place was taken by the pupils of David, by the Bousingots, the adherents of Jeune-France, and by Lord Byron. For economy's sake, the main diet hereabouts was vinegar pickles.

It goes on like that to this very day, back and forth from one terrace of refreshment to another between the Rue Saint-Benoît and the Rue Bonaparte, as if on a merry-go-round. The latter street is given over to antique dealers who, under the influence of the name, specialize in Directoire items. What is more, you may see the fantastic figure of the Bonapartist, Armand Fèvre, strutting his stuff there, attired in a redingote, armed with a knobbed cane, and wearing a top hat. Saint-Germain-des-Prés is the only place in Paris where the entire population wins name and fame spending all its time on the terraces of cafés, over a short beer. A new word has been coined to describe these little eggheads: they are called *terrassiers*. Everybody around here knows and greets everybody else, exactly as in a rural village.

Montparnasse is more reserved. When it shows itself off at the three famous cafés on the Boulevard, it is not really being itself. For that, you have to cross over to the far side of the cemetery, above the Catacombes.

These last are one of the fabulous localities of Paris. Everybody knows them but few people

There are two types of rubbernecks in Paris, or perhaps two varieties of connoisseur: those who frequent museums and those who flock the pavements. There are likewise two styles of asserting imperial sway, but only one of them confers dominion over the man in the street. We might even be in two minds about the ascendancy of the Throne. Napoleon, in the act of placing the crown on Josephine's head, commands no more rapt attention than does the sword-swallower as he urges down his prop between two puffs of his cigarette. Could it be that the one has consumed the weapon of the other?

*P*aris is not so much a place of rendezvous as a city of brief encounters ; always excepting, of course, the loving couples on the public bench der at the very thought of such oblivion, for then who would there be to ogle them ?   On the other hand, this vaguely foreign group

Not lost to the world, by any means, are the professional clotheshorses who hitch themselves to the Longchamp tallyho. They would shud-... ...esolutely through the arcades of the Palais-Royal are eager not to be admired but to be impressed.

And which, to us, should be the more engaging sight : this young girl, genuflecting in adoration before the bracelet to which she can't afford to treat herself, or the enraptured policeman, casting sheep's eyes at the pair of handcuffs of his dreams? "Alas", the disconsolate salesman in the Flea Market is thinking : "If only everyone who hankers after something had the wherewithal, business would pick up." But the fine lady, home-ward bound at midnight along the boulevards, who can afford whatever she pleases, wants nothing; she has everything already. "Oh, no, I almost forgot! I'm simply dying for a bag of peanuts..." And so the chain runs on until it is daybreak in Les Halles, where extremes meet. Here, fine-feathered night owls rub up against the hornyhanded, their medium of exchange a ready smile, their bond of union a common impulse for boiled pigs' trotters... How much can you crowd into a day in Paris? Not a great deal — yet a little of everything.

ever have been inside.   Make a few inquiries and
you will find that this is so.   In this underground
maze, nicknamed the Empire of the Dead, beneath
a sky of solid stone, you will see only skeletons,
although millions of Parisians are laid to rest in the
galleries.   There is also a fountain, the Samari-
taine, and a crude bas-relief representing the citadel
of Port-Mahon, carved by a certain Stécure.   This
quarry worker actually died in the Catacombes,
while building a flight of steps.

Montparnasse is a realm of silence.   It is full
of dairies, and of studios where discarded statues
are indecorously overgrown with moss; and one
has to be really familiar with the region in order
to find one's way into those backyards and inner
courts where the abstract and the figurative come
mysteriously into bloom.   But you will hardly
need to know French.   More likely, what you will
hear spoken is Japanese, Bengali, Urdu, Califor-
nian, or just plain slang.

What clearly meets the eye is that this whole
district, where even tradesmen are connoisseurs of
the graphic arts (take for example this modernistic
work in oils, representing the Dauthuile-Humez
title fight, which does duty as the signboard of a
café in the Rue Vercingétorix) deliberately turns its
back upon whatever is non-artistic — meaning
especially the glories of the cash box and the
sword.   Whole mountain ranges of masonry
have to be scaled to get back from here to
the wide-open spaces of the Champ-de-Mars and
the Invalides.

FÊTE NATIONALE

Take four bistros on the square,
take two pairs of shining eyes,
flags and streamers everywhere,
girl too willing, boy unwise.

Take four songs to last the night —
" Louis is the name, my pet."
Four musicians out of sight —
" Pleased to meet you.   Mine's Lucette."

Take four winds and let them blow,
dance the polka, jig, musette —
waltzers fast and waltzers slow
throng the Rue de la Roquette.

Take four street lamps burning dim —
who goes where, too gay to stop?
He with her or she with him...?
Shame!   It's time to open shop.

The districts of the Gros-Caillou and the École Militaire were laid out to serve as the great ceremonial showplace of the capital, and today they seem resigned to bear their fate. It would be hard to imagine anything more dreary than these vast avenues, too long, too broad, dustswept and dotted along with mean little vacant benches. Even the High Brass, cooped up inside their museum of old weapons, find the prospect a bore except when the outdoor carnivals come to town (this happens twice a year) and the Dip of Death and the Flying Saucers are set up there.

One does have to admit, though, that Paris can show nothing constructed with a firmer sweep of line than the Invalides.

It is hard to tell the difference, on the Champ-de-Mars, between old soldiers hobbling along and the caretakers with their pointed sticks. The children, even, seem somehow to feel this influence, forbidden as they are to shout their loudest.

But above their heads the Eiffel Tower does its balancing act, a surrealistic fish with its tail planted in the ground. What keeps it standing up? Ask the man in the street, the passing tourist, the custodians. All, without exception, will tell you that this colossal structure stands with its feet in the water and its head in the sky, like some flourishing palm tree. Even the most knowledgeable Parisians take for granted that the four pediments of the Bonickhausen Tower (for that was the real name of M. Eiffel, who lost no time in finding himself a more memorable pseudonym)

Looking for all the world like the ghost of Toulouse-Lautrec, this little man is bowlegging it down the steps of the Rue Chappe. Montmartre abounds in such gloomy backwaters, where the foaming tides of champagne leave drifters stranded. At dusk, by lamplight, it is even gloomier. One good thing about the streets of the Butte is that they all run steeply down toward the glittering promise of the boulevards where joy of living floods along the sidewalks.

Different types measure off the asphalt of Paris with different sets of compasses : seminarians with determined tread, the representative of the Law who marches " by the count ", the ribbon clerk with hurried stride. And then there are those dividers standing hither and yon with fixed legs. The one at the left, before St-Sulpice, might possibly be mistaken for the foot of Jacob's ladder, but at the right we clearly see that it is only the lamplighter's pair of steps.

The clubhouse at Longchamp. There, when gentlemen are playing hooky from the office, hard hats are de rigueur. Not so on the Butte-Montmartre where this pair of street Arabs are playing plain hooky. The first two are out after the Grand Prix. The second have left the scramble after the Prix d'Excellence to others. Burdened though they already are with nine-to-five-style briefcases, their kingdom lies elsewhere — on the handrails of the stone stairway, for instance, down which the two old railbirds never would dare to slide on the seat of their pants. " My horse for such a kingdom ! " the old sport in the black derby seems to say.

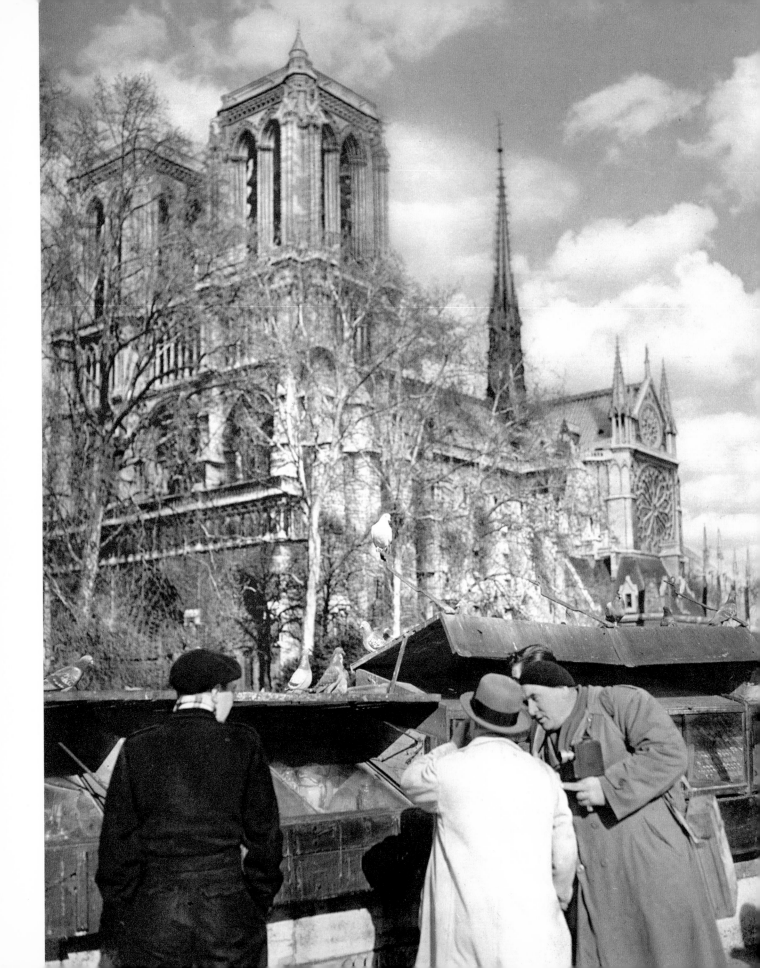

rest upon caissons full of water which serve as hydraulic jacks to hold up its enormous weight.

This lively myth dates back to the opening of the century, at which time a popular novel, *Le Scaphandrier de la Tour Eiffel*, was brought out and ran through many printings. For some obscure reason, as demanded by the involvements of the plot, the hero, dressed in a diving suit, walked down into the Seine, opened certain mysterious doors, followed along flooded passageways, and bobbed up inside the Tower from one of the afore-mentioned caissons.

So successful was this best-seller that everybody in Paris believes the tale of the Tower's fluid foundations to this very day.

According to Huysmans, Eiffel set up housekeeping in quarters on the third level of this "fretwork candle". He intended to work there. But the wind howled so loud that he came down after a single day of it, and never went up again.

The one thing you can't take away from Paris is that it was the first town ever to buy a lightning rod. From the pinnacle one descries the capital, obscured with mist, in the form of a laurel leaf with the river as its vein. The Seine is the main avenue of Paris, disputing the title with the Champs-Elysées; a peaceful thoroughfare whereon, most politely, only the *bateaux-mouches* and the fireboats contend for the right of way.

Very late at night, well past midnight, is the time to visit the Halles; and then, if fortitude and leisure serve, wait for four o'clock and the brighten-

The green coffers that heighten the parapets along the quays expose to view mysterious treasures garnered from provincial attics. Here the patient Parisian loves to come and poke through the miscellaneous objects heaped up as if by generations of mad magpies: engravings, medals, stamp collections, boarding cutlasses, ancestral helmets, and, above all, books — the great harvest of books, from which bargains may be gleaned under the critical eye of hopeful pigeons. Writers who run across their own works on display along the quays have a hard time hiding their chagrin. These coffin-shaped boxes are the tomb of many an author's last illusions. On the other hand, what more fitting fate could a " stream of consciousness " novel have than to be washed up on the bank?

emarkable piece of what
s called foreshortening.
e left, the Place de la
de with the bridge cut off,
ded by the telephoto lens;
right, the same, rendered
true perspective of its
se setting. The Hôtel
and the Ministry of
the balanced portico of
deleine, the Chamber of
s, the fringes of greenery
in from the Tuileries
and the Champs-Ély-
none of these detracts
n the least. They mere-
t off. In dead center,
or Obelisk — an out-
piece of needlework which
nt to you also in close-up,
you can make sure it is
w. For this is one of
few monuments of Paris
nnot charge admission.

ing of the sky, when the freshness of the dawn wind sharpens sight and hearing, which are rendered more susceptible to the poetry of the moment by a pleasurable fatigue. And if you should walk along the Rue Saint-Honoré under a gentle rain, it would serve only to enhance your appreciation of this vegetable-and-fruit-and-fish village at the very heart of Paris. You will find no lack of places to take shelter; *bistrots* fully as picturesque as are their names: *Le Chien qui Fume, le Cygne de la Croix, le Pied de Cochon, le Bougnat Blanc, le Chou Vert, la Poule au Pot,* where members of the night shift are sufficiently broadminded to tolerate the evening gowns and dinner jackets of the night owls.

The Halles afford never-ending astonishment. The same show goes on there every night — and every night it is a fairyland. The stage setting of this huge *opera bouffe* outdoes in sheer imaginativeness anything that the Theâtre du Châtelet could have put on display in the era of "Around the World in Twenty-Four Hours."

After so much liveliness and color, one finds the Palais-Royal an enchanting land of phantoms. The accustomed inhabitants are shadows which stir within the gloom of the colonnades. Even the shouts of velocipeding children, who nowadays have conquered this realm with their Merveilleuses and Muscadins, are all but muted under the arcade. The dealers' show cases have an indefinable, an almost occult and mesmeric drawing-power which is unique in all Paris. The shops are empty and slighlty dusty (with clean dust, of course) but they

In Paris, an outdoor carnival is never far to seek. Barkers, wrestlers, bareback riders, springing up without rhyme or reason from cracks in the pavement, announce its coming at the crossroads with a great flourish of accordions. There also are huge organized festivities which are conducted according to the strictest protocol. This is true of the Neu-Neu Festival but most notably of the Fair of the Throne. The latter has its own patent of nobility; and every year, in the Place de la Nation (the erstwhile Place du Trône), it erects a noisy amusement park flooded with arc lights where cheap pleasures and quick thrills are pepped up nowadays with diversions inspired by the atomic age and interplanetary flight. On this spot, it thus is made easy to forget, the poet André Chénier was guillotined under the Revolution.

yield up unsuspected marvels, rare and precious objects of virtu; gold medals and pewter figurines; *lettres de cachet* and jade roses. Salesmen here have the air of friendly guides, and one may go in and browse around and handle without having to buy. The shopkeepers of the Palais-Royal are collectors who love to display their treasures.

They contribute also to that suggestion of poetry imparted to this hidden garden within, where the presence of Cocteau and Colette have provided the finishing touch. "Paris from My Window" was what Colette called her weekly column; and from here she was able to glimpse it all.

As you enter the Louvre by way of the Cour Carrée, you find yourself within a stronghold constructed in the grand manner where footsteps ring agreeably upon pavements which are a pleasure to traverse. You will observe that many pedestrians, using this courtyard as a quicker means of passage from one bank to the other of the Seine, and hastening to get to their work, insensibly slow down and assume a more carefree air and take time to look up and study the circular 17th-century windows as though they were discovering a bit of some other world or corner of Paradise; a five-minute holiday.

The Tuileries Gardens ought not, actually, to differ in the least from those of the Palais-Royal. They are set about with the same stunted sort of trees along similar gravel paths, and are laid out according to the same Versailles ground plan that we owe to the Grand Siècle. But it has so chanced that,

Along the boulevards, the quick and the dead are separated by only an imaginary line. Here even the least-agile of Parisians, dodging the deadfalls in and out of traffic, squeaks through with the iron nerve of a matador. But late at night, on Pigalle, this butterfly attracted by the bright lights is all composure as the scouts attempt to net her and put her into their boîtes de nuit. In the small hours, rival nightclubs are the only deadfalls for which you have to watch out.

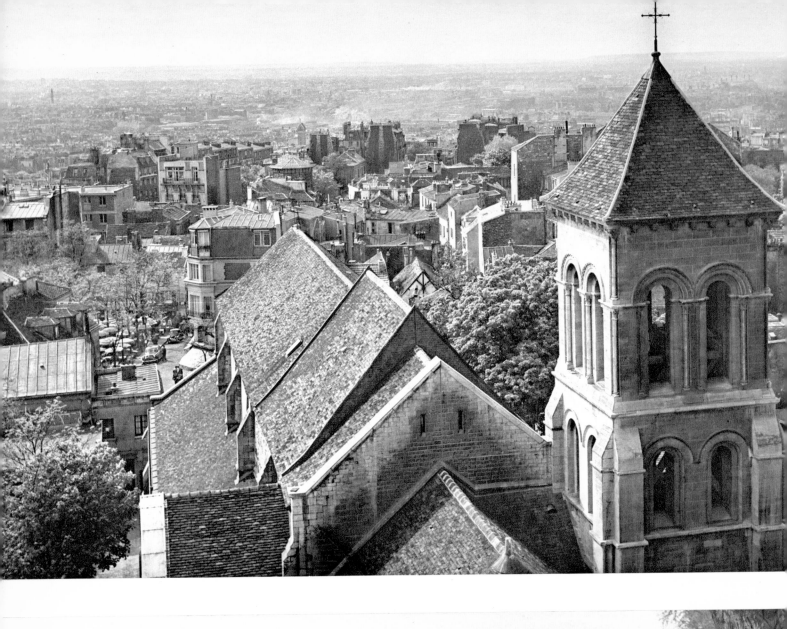

To say that Paris is made up of multiple villages has become a common-place, and the evidence tends to support it as you come in from the city gates. Then the mercers' windows become more discreet, back rooms of cafés smell of snuff and spices, last night's newspapers turn slowly yellow as they hang from their clamps in stationers' shopfronts, and the great winds that sweep the world are but a distant rumor... To the north: Montmartre, where the stepped roofs of the Eglise St-Pierre suggest a tile-roofed village. To the south: Bercy, where the asphalt cooker whistles up an out-of-work sheep dog. To the east: St-Germain de Charonne, where the street turns into a grand'rue and the old lady becomes merely une vieille. To the west: Vaugirard, where womenfolk quicken their pace along the walls when it is zero hour in the slaughterhouses.

instead of being surrounded like a patio by rectangular buildings, they are spacious and open to the fresh breezes that sweep along the margin of the Seine. The Terrasse des Feuillants and that of the Orangerie are flooded with full daylight even in midwinter. No longer is this simply a formal park in the French style, its restrained beauty evocative of royal show. It has become the setting of a pretty village festival, where marionettes act out their farce and gay-colored hobbyhorses go round and round to the whistle of calliopes. About the pool, the rising generation dreams of piracy and learns the principles that govern navigation under sail. The iron chairs are temptingly set out in couples as bait for the tender trap of love.

On the Place de la Concorde, right after twelve noon, people start queuing up at the foot of the Lille Statue. None of them pays any particular attention to this piece of sculpture. The men read newspapers and the women sit on campstools and knit. So far as the observer can tell, there is nothing to warrant this gathering; no bus stop or sideshow or notice forbidding them to proceed. Then all of a sudden the people start chattering, the pedestal shows signs of life and breaks out with a door, and the crowd disappears inside the statue. And now we can see the signboard: "Visit the Sewers of Paris!"

The Champs-Elysées is a part of Paris where it is a pleasure to stroll at any hour. The promenade is like a pretty woman, composed enough to receive admirers from dawn to dawn. But the

The beauty of Paris is to be found not alone in main-traveled streets and public squares. It lies waiting also along the encompassing hill crests, upon the heights of Montmartre or the Buttes-Chaumont, up and beyond which the city now has overflowed. René Clair, touching the rooftops of Paris with poetry, has sung of the mansards with their tiny skylights that open out amid a forest of chimney pots — but always to reveal a glimpse of some spire or belfry, or the silhouette of one of those domes which make the skyline of Paris a landmark for airborne men and migrating swallows: of the Invalides, which is gilded, and the Val de Grâce and the Sorbonne and the Institut and the Salpêtrière and, loftiest of all in altitude and aspiration, the dome of the Panthéon atop Montparnasse, where it is separated by the full sweep of the city from that huge frozen custard, the Sacré-Cœur.

*S*olid as the Pont-Neuf, the saying goes; and perishable as the stuff of daily life... From the kiosks of the Champs-Élysées to the borders of the Seine, the Parisian on his daily walk links up the transient with the eternal — though not without here and there a fruitful pause in these clamorous canyons where costermongers, solid as the Pont-Neuf, sell you provisions perishable as the passing moment. And thus you learn that the market is even more crooked than the Seine.

best time is before eleven in the morning when there is nothing to do except relish the spring air or walk the poodles or look for the materials of a scenario; or perhaps again at the close of afternoon when everyone, so to speak, is passing in review, whether to see or in order to be seen. Then café terraces, such as the renowned Fouquet's, become in effect seats on the aisle for the enjoymen- of this parade of mannequins, movie stars, clothes horses, and dowagers. Of these last, many come down the avenue by automobile, right on the sidewalk. The Cadillacs glide silently, nosing their way through the crowd; the chauffeurs wear white gloves and display that unruffled calm which is the badge of their profession; the beldames in summer give their jewels an airing, and in winter their furs, but never, never expose their makeups to the sun.

The Champs-Elysées is but one segment of the greatest municipal parkway in the world. Between the Louvre and the Rond-Point de la Défense lies a stretch of four and three-tenths miles, and along this astounding Napoleonic vista the eye leaps from the Carrousel to the Obelisk to the Arc de Triomphe.

Yet there does come a time when the Champs-Elysées takes on an unaccustomed look, or when, perhaps, it reveals its true aspect; and that is after midnight. Passers-by are few and far between, and then they are mostly ladies of the evening, loitering before darkened shop windows, pretending to price the goods they know by heart. A few men and some taxis loiter by the Lido, waiting for the

Evening on Montmartre. Here, at the cocktail hour, the very trees lean an elbow on the zinc of some favorite roof and murmur, " Am I bushed ! "

girls to come out. But farther down, past the Rond-Point, there lies a sort of Robin Hood's dell, a grotesque garden composed of blobs of black leafage and bluish globes that glow like eerie blossoms; and through the shadows prowl men with a furtive appearance and women of questionable intent. Lovers no longer have the benches to themselves.

Which brings to mind how the nude corpse of the Sieur Lebon was found in a Paris thicket, stabbed in thirty-six places, on the night of Napoleon's coronation. Lebon was well known as the man who had proposed a crackpot scheme for lighting the town with jets of gas. He had spent his life crusading against the darkness of Paris streets, only to fall victim to the cause of his complaint. Not until eleven years later, in 1815, did Parisians touch off the first gaslight.

The Bois de Boulogne is all that remains to us of the Forest of Rouvray, but it is a lovely remnant. Like a flower in the buttonhole, it puts the final touch to the elegance of Paris. It is dense enough so that people can get lost in it, and they most reprehensibly shoot the pigeons, and as for what they wear, the less said the better, but the margins of the lakes are indescribably appealing, remote from the tumult of the town. The great bridle paths remain still the same as when Proust went in search, there, of a certain young bud in the unfolding of her charm, and one might suppose them to be desert sandtracks marked out by the passage of unseen caravans. In the Jardin d'Acclimata-

The Palais de Chaillot still passes under the name of its progenitor, which was called the Trocadéro. That was a black-browed building with projecting, ugly features and a bulbous nose. When the offspring made its appearance at the Exposition of 1937, Parisians raised a cheer. They were less pleased when it grew a little wart to signalize the " provisional " installation of a U. N. meeting place. Like everything that is provisional under the sun, what was set up in the guise of a temporary excrescence is fast becoming eternal. Wherefore, when the discriminating wish to admire the expanse of the Palais de Chaillot, they climb the Eiffel Tower and look down on it.

Victory, so hi
teaches, is lik
make you lose your
Perhaps the W.
Victory of Samot
lost her own dow
grand stairway o,
Louvre, as the litt.
on the Luxem
steps is determine
to lose her ball –
determined, that
gives wings to her a

tion, the zebus are standoffish and no longer cause excitement except to the children. Parents, on the other hand, are delighted to have their offspring as an excuse for climbing blissfully aboard the tiny yellow train that departs from the Porte Maillot.

On the farther side, to the west, the Boulevards converge toward the hub of Parisian railway activity where, at Saint-Lazare, the names of virtually all the capitals of Europe come together in a traffic jam. The Cours de Rome and du Havre are crucial points of an interminable guerilla war between pedestrians and motorists; nor is there any end in sight to this rivalry between the fleet but fragile bipeds and the awkward but terrifying quadriwheels. It would seem as though two species of animals were contending for possession of a jungle trail. One faction, scurrying upon tiny paws, moves with the silly speed of newsreels of the year 1900; heads down, the members of the other scuttle over the ground like great shiny black beetles, bulling their way along. The reason for this unending struggle is not known. It has been observed, however, that the metal-bodied insects nearly always come out on top, while the perpendicular vertebrates give up and flee back to the refuge of the métro, as their system of underground burrows is called. As a last resort, they may have to take cover in the Salle des Pas-Perdus — almost the only place of shelter that remains to them for the pursuit of their brief amours.

The Opéra, around which a wholly different Paris pivots — the city of big business and light

n the foreground, the Lycée Henri IV; center, St-Etienne-du-Mont; background, the Ecole Polytechnique; not own, the Bibliothèque Ste-Geneviève. rom Clovis to Napoleon, the university uarter is a history of France compiled in one. Toy soldiers, tricked out with corne and sword, plow their way bravely rough it. They are the Polytechnicians, hose hope it is to prolong that history in sh and blood: for they are France's ture. A future which is already in the ust — or so the ill-disposed are pleased say. But they only half believe it.

The derelict [...]
sues no [...]
eer. Flat on [...]
back in the sh[...]
of a hoist, he s[...]
with the curb[...]
for pillow. O[...]
has "a little s[...]
thing going [...]
him", an ever[...]
ing gamble, [...]
ning from one y[...]
end to the [...]
which never [...]
off. It does [...]
matter. Wit[...]
hat pulled [...]
over his eyes [...]
precaution ag[...]
having to loo[...]
future in the [...]
he has turned [...]
back on happ[...]
for good and [...]

Grand Hôtel is caravansary where travelers go in one door and out another, like idle words through a heedless head. And the Rue Scribe has preserved just enough character so that when one sees a man enter that hotel burdened with a raincoat and haversacks, one has the impression that there goes Phineas Fogg, making up for lost time on his trip around the world in eighty days. The cafés are merely vast goldfish bowls which reduce the patrons to the semblance of dolls in a diorama. Even the Musée Grévin is simply a crowded waiting room for people made of wax. People swarm the Boulevards, but obviously no one lives there.

Only out at their eastern end, toward Bonne-Nouvelle, do the Boulevards take on an aspect of normal life. Around the Portes Saint-Denis and Saint-Martin, which can be bypassed without sparing them a glance, flourishes a noisy hive which seemingly has taken in the displaced population from the center. The Rues Saint-Denis and Saint-Martin, which run past the arches of triumph not only in order to change their names but also to gain a quality slightly reminiscent of the old time nobility of the Faubourgs, drain away toward the north into the Rues des Petites-Écuries and des Récollets, where their character peters out.

Here, though, the Great Age of the Theatre still is respectfully enough recalled so that the Café Battifol, at the head of the Faubourg Saint-Martin, caters to a clientele of theatre folk exclusively, old dudes and madwomen of Chaillot, has-been tenors and wrinked soubrettes — a world in itself of

It would be fun to suppose that when the clock in the Senate Chamber signals that it is time to take a break, the Councilors of the Republic come running out to the Luxembourg pool and sail paper boats there. But no such thing. These yachts, tacking and reaching on their scale-model cruises, have skippers in short pants; and this garden remains, beneath the presumptive long white beards of our Patres conscripti, a green paradise for the gamboling of puppy love. Outgrowing puppy love, the handsome dogs proceed to sun themselves beside the pool of the Tuileries where, playing harder to get than a touch of summer tan, they spark beneath a screen of stern indifference.

The king of beasts on the terrace of the Tuileries is a cowardly lion. On the Pointe du Vert-Galant, the celebrated white horse of Henri IV turns greener and greener, while atop the Grand-Palais the steeds of Immortality's chariot gallop ever faster in their race to outstrip Time; and on the Pont de Grenelle the statue of Liberty, scaled down to more intimate proportions than the one at New York, is thawing the ice with her torch... These are not to be mistaken for mere snapshots. They are such sidelong traits of Paris as we momentarily glimpse out of the corner of an eye, when works of art may be caught in the act of leading their own lives.

ringing voices and beautiful diction, of fake jewels and sweeping gestures.

It is colder along the Rue Saint-Martin than anywhere else in Paris. Residents confirm this; and the reason may be the canal. In the Tenth Arrondissement, one never says "Canal Saint-Martin", any more than one would say "Canal de l'Ourcq" out beyond Jaurès. One simply says The Canal — what other could there be? A suggestion of Venice overhangs this highly distinctive region, prolific as it is of human-interest stories, of crimes of passion in the rainy night, and lovesick girls for whom the passing barges keep a weather eye out. And a single book, it well may be, is responsible, setting the tone for a half-mile of waterway : *Hôtel du Nord* by Eugène Dabit. Not a week goes by but what some timid stranger applies for a room at that famous hostelry; which has taken, however, the precaution of changing its name.

The Quartier du Marais has the look of a peaceful, rosy oasis. Here all the streets encircle the former Place Royale — renamed Place des Vosges in 1793, in tribute to the first taxpayers of the Republic who met their quota — as if the whole neighborhood were an idle merry-go-round. This unassuming square has arcaded galleries like a monastery where there is always time to gossip and conjure up the past. Victor Hugo and Mme de Sévigné still live here. One can express it no other way... they are immortal. You may visit their apartments while they are out, touch their

The Pont-Royal, *built under Louis XIV, is considered by those who have viewed it at twilight to be the handsomest bridge in Paris; for at that hour its arches and their precise reflections imaged in the calm water form perfect circles. The stately presence of the Louvre adds to the brooding felicity of the scene, which owes its charm no less to history than to geometry.*

The Cour Carrée of the Louvre is a short-cut which Parisians freely use in order to reach the heart of the Right Bank from the quays. For many, it is like indulging in a moment of grandeur to pass before these galleries where the centuries put forth a hand or jog one's elbow. And here the grandeur is not simply a matter of mere proportions which make this the hugest palace in the world. It resides in the significance of the finished work, whose vast elaboration bears witness to a sort of relay of endeavor, in the course of which the best exponents of French taste have handed on the torch to one another down the ages. A dungeon under Philippe-Auguste, a fortress under Charles V an airy chateau under François I, the Louvre was closed down as a royal residence under Louis XIV, served Napoleon I as a ceremonial palace, and stands today as the sole monument wherein every style of architecture blends happily with all the rest; where the successive régimes of France appear to have linked their efforts into a harmonious sequence of accord.

furniture, sniff his pipe smoke and the scent of her perfume vials.

Happily, the banks of the Seine at this point remain unchanged. They still are as they wer- when Pissarro and Signac put them on canvas; so much so, that you find yourself wondering whether nature has not copied art. The barges here lie packed against the quayside like a log jam, painted in pleasing shades of rust-red and burgundy. From the Quai des Célestins the most restful land-scape in all Paris may be viewed; it is the Ile Saint-Louis, favored by fishermen, who always have good taste and often cut shoots from the poplars in preference to their bamboo rods.

The Bastille remains still to be taken, judging by the strong attraction it exercises upon Parisians. Tradition requires that they go slumming down in the Rue de Lappe by way of celebrating the Four-teenth of July.

The *fête nationale* is essentially a Parisian holi-day. It is to Paris what the Carnival is to Rio and the Festival to Venice. Amorous encounters, while it lasts, begin and end as family affairs. It is a mass ritual of love-making; our equivalent of Midsummer Night. Persons under the influence of familiar spirits then fall readily from grace — if not too gracefully. Husbands make passes at their wives and wives make off to their lovers. Every-body vanishes for a moment up dark alleys. And a long moment it is before he or she comes back, with rumpled hair and his or her mouth a smear of lipstick, exclaiming, "Oh, *there* you are! Which

Since motor buses first came into us
they have undergone repeated alter-
tions of the hemline, as it were, greatly
the distress of the Parisians, who are ve
fond of them and refer to them familiar
as " my bus ". By way of compensatio
the fiacres never change, but, like son
species of animals, they are well on the
way to becoming extinct. Landaus, ca
riolets, and phaetons are the last of t
dinosaurs, forlornly roaming the trails
the asphalt jungle, whence they can
lured by particularly pretty girls who ha
a world of time on their hands and may fe
a momentary impulse for cutting a dash.
Here we see the coachman brightly smili
to hide the fact that he is deaf, while t
horse turns both ears to catch the addres
which it will be up to him to remembe

way did you go? I've been hunting for you, for an hour...!" It is a great night to be alive.

But in the course of this diversion we have lost track of the Bastille; nor do the drought-stricken dancers, for the most part, know what became of it. Not any more than is known what was ever done with the three baldheaded men and the man with cropped hair, those four dumbfounded prisoners whom the people of 1789 released from their cells. Even the traffic cop at the foot of the Boulevard Beaumarchais was unable to tell me exactly where the fortress used to stand. Right there, in the Place de la Bastille, the outlines of the moat are indicated on the pavement. If you want to track them down among the buses, go ahead and risk your neck!

On Pigalle, in the blinding neon glare of night-spot advertising ("Floor Show," it says on every side; meaning what?), you may take doormen and barkers at their word when they promise you, with frantic shouts, the most daring nudes in the world. Total undress can apparently be carried to extremes. Men without women furtively cast sidelong glances at the photos in full color which have lately gone on display — little semi-opaque aquariums let into the fronts of *boîtes de nuit* are flooded with ultramarine light, wherein bare-bosomed cuties may be seen swimming in the pale-pink larval phase.

Except on Saturday nights, though, Montmartre has not changed since Utrillo. In spite of all, the Butte retains a peculiar charm. You have to regard it as a national park, an extra-territorial

"Won't someone rescue me?" cries this young girl who has been turned into a pillar of salt for attempting to visit the Hôtel de Sens during an off hour. All the props of a fairytale are here at hand — haunted castle, heavy chains, on the bough a bird's nest full of snowflakes — so that the more you look, the more you wonder whether Snow White is waiting for a taxi or Prince Charming.

yclist in the act of shov-
off from the Place de
de Ville has one of the
obs in Paris.   He is the
who delivers the world
your doorstep while the
still so hot that it burns
d like loaves fresh from
floor.   He is called a
ujours.   His presence
is proverbial and he
w to whistle through his
Thanks to these endow-
e darts at will through
g surf of "les grands
ds".   But even his skill
when he comes to this
ment in the Place Cli-
re those who own no
an work off their repress-
s for catastrophe at the
tiny crash cars. Be-
eir bumpers not even a
could slip.

possession of Paris, where specimens of whatever the city has been able to produce in the way of ancient houses, rustic streets, patches of greenery, and weedy little pavements are preserved. The Butte remains a thinly disguised museum, the only difference being that it features live exhibits : painters straight out of Murger's novels, village constables, ragamuffins without pants who belong in the Chamber of Horrors, and the whole series of "mayors". There is plenty of fakery in all this but it is so playfully done that one overlooks the fraud.

The Butte is our sole surviving reminder of the days of inn-yard cafés, of bonnets tossed over the windmill (de la Galette) and love under a hedge and orgies on homemade wine. Most of the streets of Montmartre are standing up well under the steady erosion of rubber-tired tourist pilgrimages. The old main street of the upper village, the Rue Saint-Rustique, is reserved for nuns; and walls overtopped with green boughs along the Rue de l'Abreuvoir conceal enchanted gardens where statues pine away.

The line of windmills, that is the hillcrests, runs off to the northeast of Paris by way of the peaks of Belleville and Ménilmontant and terminates at the Butte de Montreuil, that remarkable above-ground quarry. It mud-caked trails, where no one ever goes any more except kids on the warpath and daredevil motorcyclists, dip and rise like the tracks of a scenic railway. In former years, the people of Ménilmontant and Belleville never bothered to come down to Paris except for the big

In Paris, the bloom gets rubbed off young..." (Breffort).

Hideaway for lovers, *museum for artists, cabaret for sporting types, graveyard for the dead, palace for kings, hangout for tramps, Paris is also the rookery of a teeming day-to-day life where one generation passes along to the next, without half seeming even to try, the art of living hale and eating hearty.*

binge at Courtille on Shrove Tuesday. And often the young fry, even yet, have never seen the Seine and know the Eiffel Tower only from postcards. Nowadays, this tribal disrespect has backfired upon the natives. Parisians, leaving what they call the Paris hinterland to stagnate, never set foot in these peripheral villages.

From the plateau of the Envierges, however, a clearer view of Paris may be obtained than from the Sacré-Cœur, where the ridge is only six feet higher. Here, the gradient is so steep that the hillside hutments tumble one upon another and it takes a strong pair of legs to gain the top of the endless flights of steps. When a child's ball gets away from her up there, she needs an hour to retrieve it. Every so often, as you go up, rubber balls will pass you like toy balloons escaping in reverse, bounding from street to street in ever longer arcs, and roof to roof, clear down to the belfry of Saint-Eupatoria.

Along the fringes of this submarginal zone there is nothing else to see except the flea markets. Since the old one at Mouffetard was shut down, you have to go to Clignancourt in particular, or else to Montreuil and Vanves, if you care to view that artless exhibition and pick up odd items for a song.

The circuit of Paris closes, in my opinion, at the foot of the Boulevard Victor, where the Porte de Bas-Meudon leads under the Auteuil Viaduct, at which point you can start your explorations all over again and never weary of them.

When speaking of the picturesque aspects of our city, there is a reprehensible habit of running

In such a twilight on the Champs-Él sées, earth and sky appear to seal grand alliance. Overhead are blended t pastel tones of the Ile-de-France, while our feet the Milky Way goes streaming b The serpentining red of traffic running to the Etoile and the twisting gold of t current coming down might serve as er blems of a bloodstream old as the world men, yet ever renewed. This is the ho when the Arc de Triomphe comes triu phantly into its own — when, aglow wit radiance which is like a consecration, stands revealed as simply the open door friendship and good will.

down the present in favor of the past. In 1956, people are disappointed not to find the red-light districts that used to give the town the flavor of some exotic port of call. In the middle of the 19th century, however, newspapers already were saying that Paris had seen its best days. Vandalism, they called it, viewing the process of "Haussmannization" with alarm; and they mourned for the bewildering mare's nest of labyrinthine passageways and jolting cobbles that the capital used to be before the great avenues went through. Then came the Exposition of 1900, plunging Paris into an era of unsettling "modernism." After the 1914 war, people sighed for the Age of Elegance. And in 1939 they were waxing nostalgic over the good old days of the Bœuf sur le Toit... At the rate things are going now, you may count on it that in 1970 people will look back upon our mid-century scene with misty eyes as they recall the quick-lunch counters with rippling neon signs, the liquor ads, vending machines, pretty arsenic-green buses, gasoline-perfumed taxis, and the cemeteries right in the heart of town... for *these* are the good old days of times to come.

JEAN-PAUL CLÉBERT.

Fall 1956

This picture belongs to the general inheritance. Except in the sense that the Capital is custodian of the greater part of the national heritage, the scene is not Parisian. The flame that for thirty-six years has burned under the Arc de Triomphe night and day is a vigil lamp for all of France, just as the soldier who sleeps beneath this entablature of bronze is a mute summons to soul-searching for us all. And today there is a whole generation of men now fully grown who more or less keenly feel themselves to be the true-born sons of this unknown father.

If Paris is doomed
become one day a
city under a stormy
here is how she will
mild and sheeplike, p
fied in the act of
about her business...

e sky over Paris,
loveliest in the
and the most
tinted, calls
e play of light-
er than the thun-
And the Eif-
r, be it hideous
ome, stands like
ic paper weight
he city battened
ainst every gale.

The world's to blame if, in our humdrum day,
the charms of fair Lutetia fade away:
Paris! whom Victor Hugo's firm decree,
echoed by many from beyond the sea,
once named the heir of Rome,
the mundane pilgrim's home away from home
queen of the arts and high civility.
Gone is the myth of Paris the young bride,
to each a virgin though by all men tried.
This hard-boiled era with its carping stress
on knowing more and more of less and less
rejects the legend. Yet the fact remains
(or question, rather, teasing one-track brains):
Can such a city, warmed by its own friction,
hope still to thrive, a living contradiction?
A city scornful of efficiency,
mistrustful of production en série,
but unresigned to be the gilded heap
where lion and lizard keep
their deathwatch on the stale necrophily
of a museum? A metropolis
where science yields a warm esthetic bliss?
A town where problems of technique and taste,
to plumb the universe or drape and baste
a swatch of bolt goods, rouse an equal passion:
Can such a town survive the reigning fashion
for grinding faces and produce—trash?
It can. It does; and when the tawdry, brash,
and dull imbalance of a world at odds
with reason, laughter, and the household gods
has come full circle, here will Paris be,
undimmed, the mirror of mankind
where all who look may find,
now grave now gay, the face of memory.

TWO THOUSAND YEARS OF PARIS
CHRONOLOGY BY YVAN CHRIST

53 B. C.

Cæsar appoints *Lutetia Parisiorum* as meeting place of deputies from the people of Gaul.

52 B. C.

First battle of Paris: LABIENUS, Cæsar's lieutenant, crushes revolt of Parisii under CAMULOGENUS.

First and 2nd centuries

A Gallo-Roman town develops on Mt. Sainte-Geneviève and the Ile de la Cité.

c. 150 A. D.

Construction of the " Palais des Thermes " of Cluny (Collegium Nautæ Parisiaci, or merchant boatmen of the Seine ?)

3rd century

Martyrdom of SAINT-DENIS, missionary and first Bishop of Paris.

c. 250

Invasion of Germanic tribes destroys the Roman quarter on the Right Bank.

360

JULIAN THE APOSTATE proclaimed Emperor by his army in the Roman palace on the Cité.

451

During the invasion by ATTILA, Ste GENEVIÈVE forbids the Parisians to flee.

Beginning of the 6th century

Documentary references to Saint-Étienne-de-la-Cité, first cathedral of Paris, predecessor of Notre-Dame.

507

CLOVIS founds the Abbey of Sts. Peter and Paul (Sainte-Geneviève).

508

He makes Paris the seat of his realm.

c. 542

Foundation by Childebert I of the Abbaye Saint-Vincent and Sainte-Croix (Saint-Germain-des-Prés).

c. 586

Paris burns. The Merovingians and then the Carlovingians abandon the town in favor of Aix-la-Chapelle.

885

The Normans lay siege to the city, defended by Bishop GOZLIN and ODO, Count of Paris (founder of the Capetian line), who is proclaimed king in 887.

987

Accession of Hugh Capet. Paris the capital once more.

990-1014

Belfry of Saint-Germain-des-Prés goes up.

Start of the 12th century

GUILLAUME DE CHAMPEAUX and ABÉLARD are teaching in the cloister schools of Notre-Dame.

1121

Louis VI grants monopoly to *Parisian river merchants*.

1147

Pope EUGENIUS III, attended by Saint Bernard, consecrates Saint-Pierre de Montmartre.

1163

Bishop MAURICE DE SULLY starts construction of Notre-Dame Cathedral.
Pope INNOCENT III consecrates Saint-Germain-des-Prés.

1183

PHILIP AUGUSTUS orders the Halles to be built on site of the Champeaux Market established under Louis VII.

1190-1210

He builds a new wall around Paris with the Louvre as its western limit.

1200

He lays the foundation of the University.

1214

FERRAND Count of Flanders, defeated at Bouvines by Philip Augustus and imprisoned in the keep of the Louvre.

First quarter of the 13th century

PERROTIN-LE-GRAND, choirmaster of Notre-Dame, composes the first polyphonic motets.

c. 1245-1250

Completion of Notre-Dame.

1246-1248

SAINT LOUIS orders construction (by PIERRE DE MONTREUIL ?) of the Sainte-Chapelle.

1256

SAINT THOMAS AQUINAS writes his " Summa Theologiæ " in the Dominican monastery in the Rue Saint-Jacques.
ROBERT DE SORBON founds the Sorbonne.

1268

Étienne Boileau, provost of the merchants, publishes the " Livre des Métiers ", summarizing rules of trade and labor regulations.

after 1276

Jean de Meung continues " The Romance of the Rose " begun by Guillaume de Lorris.

close of the 13th and start of the 14th centuries

Reconstruction of the Palais Royal de la Cité and the Conciergerie.

1308-1312

Philipe le Bel suppresses the Knights Templar.

1358

First revolution in Paris. Étienne Marcel, provost of the merchants, institutes a reign of terror and is assassinated by Jean Maillard.

1360-1370

Charles V rebuilds and amplifies the Louvre; installs the King's Library there.

1367

Hugues Aubriot, provost of the merchants, begins new city wall with the Bastille as its eastern limit.

1382

Revolt of the Maillotins: massacre of tax collectors and Jewish money lenders; debtors freed from jail.

1402

Charles VI authorizes the " Confrérie de la Passion " to put on plays inspired by Holy Writ.

1407

Assassination of the Duc d'Orléans. Paris in the hands of the Burgundian faction.

1413

Led by Caboche, the Butchers' Guild issues proclamations of mob rule.

1420

December 1st: Henry V, King of England and heir to the Throne of France by terms of Treaty of Troyes, enters Paris; start of enemy occupation.

1429

September 8: Joan of Arc, attempting to free Paris, wounded outside the Porte Saint-Honoré.

1430

December 16: Henry VI, King of France and England, crowned in Notre-Dame.

1436

August 15: Paris freed from English occupation.

1437

Charles VII makes his entry into Paris.

c. 1450

The " True Mystery of the Passion " by Arnoul Greban, choirmaster of Notre-Dame, first presented in Paris at the Hôpital de la Trinité.

1455

November 7: Institution at Notre-Dame of formal procedure of rehabilitation of Joan of Arc.

1456

François Villon writes his " Petit Testament "

1470

Gering, Freiburger and Creutz, pupils of Gutenberg, inaugurate printing at the College of the Sorbonne.

1474-1519

Construction of the Hôtel of the Archbishops of Sens.

1485-1498

Construction of the Hôtel of the Monks of Cluny.

1495

Completion of Saint-Séverin.

1508-1522

Construction of the belfry of Saint-Jacques-de-la-Boucherie (the Tour Saint-Jacques).

1532

Foundation of the Collège de France by Francis I.

1533

Laying of cornerstone of Hôtel de Ville, built by Le Broccador.

1546

Francis I commissions Pierre Lescot to rebuild the Louvre.

1549

Jean Goujon designs the Fontaine des Innocents.
Manifesto of the Pléiade : Du Bellay publishes his " Défense et Illustration de la langue Française. "

1557

First Reformed Consistory founded in Paris by Jean Le Maçon.

1559

Marriage of Francis II and Mary Stuart at the Louvre.

1564

Catherine de' Medici commissions Philibert de l'Orme to build the Tuileries.

1572

August 24: Massacre of Saint Bartholomew's Day.

1578

Henri III lays cornerstone of the Pont-Neuf, completed under Henry IV.

1588

May 12: The " Holy Catholic League " organizes the " Day of the Barricades ". HENRI III leaves Paris for Saint-Cloud, where he is assassinated the year after.

1594

March 22: Entry of HENRI IV into Paris.   Te Deum in Notre-Dame.

1595-1610

Construction of the Grande Galerie of the Louvre by LOUIS MÉTEZEAU and JACQUES II ANDROUET DU CERCEAU.

1605

Construction of the Place Royal (subsequently Place des Vosges).

1610

May 14: Assassination of HENRI IV by RAVAILLAC, rue de la Ferronnerie.

1614

Commissioning of CHRISTOPHE MARIE, a contractor, to build and develop the Ile Saint-Louis.

1615-1625

SALOMON DE BROSSE builds the Luxembourg for Marie de' Medici.

1626

RICHELIEU commissions LE MERCIER to remodel the Sorbonne.

1627

FATHER DERAND starts construction of the Jesuit church, Saint-Paul-Saint-Louis.

1628

The Marquise de RAMBOUILLET opens her " Salon " to receive the leaders of society and letters.

1631

THÉOPHRASTE RENAUDOT issues first number of " La Gazette ".

1634

RICHELIEU founds the Académie Française.

1636

First performance of CORNEILLE's " LE CID " at the Théâtre du Marais.

1643

MOLIÈRE founds " L'Illustre Théâtre ", rue de Seine.

1645

LOUIS XIV lays cornerstone of the Val-de-Grâce, built by FRANÇOIS MANSART.

1648

LE BRUN prompts founding of the Académie de Peinture et de Sculpture.

1648-1652

La Fronde (Civil wars).

1657

Publication of the " LETTRES PROVINCIALES " of PASCAL.

1661

MOLIÈRE moves his theater into the Palais-Royal. MAZARIN establishes the Collège des Quatre Nations (the Institut), built by LE VAU.

1662

The first common carriers, suggested by PASCAL, are put into operation for a few years. A joyous tournament (carrousel), led by LOUIS XIV, takes place between the Louvre and Tuileries, celebrating birth of the Grand Dauphin. Establishment of the Gobelin Factory.

1664

LE VAU and D'ORBLAY commissioned to remodel the Tuileries. LE NÔTRE lays out the Gardens, the Avenue des Champs-Élysées, and the Place de l'Étoile.

1667

Creation of the post of Lieutenant of Police.

1668

Colonnade of the Louvre built by PERRAULT, LE VAU, and LE BRUN.

1669

Louis XIV establishes the Opéra.

1670

He founds the Hôtel des Invalides, built by LIBÉRAL BRUANT.

1673

Death of MOLIÈRE at close of fourth presentation of his " Malade Imaginaire ". First performance of LULLY's " Cadmus et Hermione ".

1677

First performance of RACINE's " Phèdre "

1679

JULES HARDOUIN-MANSART starts work on the dome of the Invalides.

1680

Louis XIV founds the Comédie-Française.

1682

He transfers the Court to Versailles.

1685

Laying of cornerstone of the Pont-Royal, built by JULES HARDOUIN-MANSART and JACQUES IV GABRIEL.

1687

BOSSUET pronounces funeral oration of the GRAND CONDÉ in Notre-Dame.

1699

JULES HARDOUIN-MANSART builds the Place Vendôme.
First annual Exhibition of the Académie de Peinture et de Sculpture (the future " Salon ") held in the Grande Galerie of the Louvre.

1705-1709

DELAMAIR builds the Palais Soubise (Archives Nationales).

1719-1720

The South Sea Bubble.

1720

WATTEAU paints " L'Enseigne de Gersaint ".

1721

MONTESQUIEU publishes " Les Lettres Persanes ".

1732

Closing of the Saint-Médard Cemetery, scene of Jansenist agitation by the " Convulsionnaires ".

1733

First performance of RAMEAU's " Hippolyte et Aricie ".

1733-1745

SERVANDONI constructs the façade of Saint-Sulpice.

1742

BOUCHER exhibits " Diane Sortant du Bain ".

1751

Publication of the first volume of the Encyclopedia.

1752-1757

J. A. GABRIEL builds the Ecole Militaire.

1754

He builds the Place Louis XIV (la Concorde).

1761

CHARDIN exhibits " La Pourvoyeuse ".

1762

Parliament issues decree for ROUSSEAU's arrest, following publication of " Emile ".

1764

CONTANT D'IVRY begins construction of the Madeleine.
LOUIS XV lays cornerstone of the Church of Sainte-Geneviève (the Panthéon), built by SOUFFLOT.

1770

Marriage of the Dauphin and MARIE ANTOINETTE; 132 persons crushed to death in the Place Louis XV during festivities.

1774

First performance of GLUCK's " Orpheus ".

1778

" Apothéose " of VOLTAIRE at the Comédie-Française, then installed in the Tuileries.

1783

Balloon ascension from the Champ-de-Mars.

1784

First performance of " The Marriage of Figaro " by BEAUMARCHAIS,
Building of Palais-Royal completed by VICTOR LOUIS.

1789

July 14: Taking of the Bastille.
October 6: The King returns to Paris.

1790

July 14: Fête de la Fédération.

1792

August 10: Revolt of Paris and seizure of the Tuileries.

1793

January 21: Execution of LOUIS XVI.
Opening of the Grande Galerie of the Louvre as converted into a museum.

1794

9 Thermidor: Fall of Robespierre.

1797

Destruction of the Church of Saint-Jacques-de-la-Boucherie.

1800

BONAPARTE First Consul; he enters the Tuileries.

1801

A Consular decree orders the creation of the Rue de Rivoli, the work of PERCIER and FONTAINE.

1802

CHATEAUBRIAND publishes his " Génie du Christianisme ".

1803

Opening of the Pont des Arts.

1804

NAPOLÉON I crowned in Notre-Dame by Pius VII.

1805-1807

DAVID at work on " The Coronation of Napoléon ".

1806

CHALGRIN starts work on the Arc de Triomphe de l'Etoile.
PERCIER and FONTAINE build the Arc de Triomphe du Carrousel.

1806-1810

Erection of the Vendôme Column.

1808

Prud'hon exhibits " La Justice et la Vengeance Divine Poursuivant le Crime ".

1814-1815

The Allies enter Paris. Restoration of Louis XVIII. The Hundred Days. Second Restoration of the Bourbons.

1815

Publication of Béranger's first collection of songs.

1820

Lamartine publishes " Les Méditations ".

1822

Victor Hugo publishes " Odes et Ballades ".

1827

Ingres exhibits " L'Apothéose d'Homère ".

1830

The July Monarchy: Abdication of Charles X and accession of Louis-Philippe.
Stendhal publishes " Le Rouge et le Noir ", Musset " Les Contes d'Espagne et d'Italie ".
" The Battle of Hernani " at the Comédie-Française.
First performance of Berlioz' " Symphonie Fantastique ".

1831

Daumier publishes his first lithographs of political types.

1835

Opening of the railway between Paris and Saint-Germain.
Balzac publishes " Le Père Goriot ".

1836

Place de la Concorde remodeled by Hittorf; installation of the Obelisk of Luxor.
Dedication of the Arc de Triomphe de l'Etoile.

1839

The daguerreotype described by Arago before the Académie des Sciences.

1840

December 15: Second funeral of Napoleon.

1842

Church of the Madeleine completed.

1845

Restoration of Notre-Dame undertaken by Lassus and carried out by Viollet-le-Duc.

1848

February 22-24: Revolution; abdication of Louis-Philippe.
Proclamation of the Second Republic.
June 23-26: Revolt of the workers.

1851

December 2 : Coup d'Etat of Louis-Napoléon.
Courbet exhibits " Un Enterrement à Ornans ".

1852

The Second Empire.

1852-1857

The Louvre completed by Visconti and Lefuel.

1852-1858

The Bois de Boulogne deeded to the city; landscaped by Alphand.

1853

Haussmann becomes Prefect of the Seine; he and Napoléon III plan the boulevard system of Paris.

1854

Decree authorizing completion of the Place de l'Etoile, with buildings to be designed by Hittorf.

1854-1866

Baltard builds the Halles.

1855

First Exposition Universelle.
Formation of the Compagnie Générale des Omnibus.

1857

Baudelaire publishes " Les Fleurs du Mal ".

1858

First performance of Offenbach's " Orphée aux Enfers ".

1861

First performance of Gounod's " Faust ".

1861-1875

Construction of the Opéra by Charles Garnier.

1863

Manet exhibits " Le Déjeuner sur l'Herbe ".

1867

Exposition Universelle.
Opening of the Parc des Buttes-Chaumont, designed by Alphand.

1870

September 4: Proclamation of the Third Republic in the Hôtel de Ville.
September 19-January 28: Siege of Paris. The Germans occupy the capital for three days.

1871

March 18-May 28: The Commune.
Burning of the Tuileries, Hôtel de Ville, Palais de Justice and Palais-Royal.
The Vendôme Column pulled down.
Zola begins publication of the " Rougon-Macquart ".

1874

First Impressionist Exhibition. VERLAINE publishes " Romances sans Paroles ".

1874-1882

Hôtel de Ville rebuilt by BALLU and DEPERTHES.

1875

ABADIE starts construction of the Basilica of the Sacré-Cœur.

1877

First performance of BIZET's " Carmen "; of " Samson et Dalila " by SAINT-SAENS.
RENOIR exhibits " Le Moulin de la Galette ".
MALLARMÉ publishes " L'Après-midi d'un Faune ".

1878

Exposition Universelle.

1885

Funeral of VICTOR HUGO.

1886

VAN GOGH arrives in Paris.
RIMBAUD publishes " Illuminations ".

1889

Exposition Universelle.
General Boulanger's " attempt ".
Construction of the Eiffel Tower.
TOULOUSE-LAUTREC does the scenery for " La Baraque de la Goulue "

1890

BRANLY reports the first results of his research in wireless telegraphy to the Académie des Sciences.

1891

First automobile race, Paris to Brest.

1894

Condemnation of Captain DREYFUS. Beginning of the " Affair ".
ANATOLE FRANCE publishes " Le Lys Rouge ".

1895

First showing of LUMIÈRE's cinematograph in the basement of the Grand Café.

1897

GIDE publishes " Les Nourritures Terrestres ".
GUIMART builds the " Castel Béranger "; birth of " modern " architecture.

1898

First Automobile Show.
HUYSMANS publishes " La Cathédrale ".

1899

The Métropolitain is built.
PIERRE CURIE discovers radium.

1900

Exposition Universelle.
DEGLANE builds the Grand-Palais and GIRAULT the Petit-Palais.
PICASSO arrives in Paris.
COLETTE publishes " Claudine à l'Ecole ".
First performance of CHARPENTIER's " Louise ".
First performance of ROSTAND's " L'Aiglon ".

1902

First performance of DEBUSSY's " Peléas et Mélisande ".

1903

EDWARD VII visits Paris. Resumption of the Entente Cordiale.

1905

Fauvism (MATISSE, MARQUET, DERAIN, VLAMINCK) at the Salon d'Automne.

1907

BERGSON publishes " L'Evolution Créatrice ".

1910

The Seine floods the lower quarters.
PÉGUY publishes " Le Mystère de la Charité de Jeanne d'Arc ".
First performance of RAVEL's " Daphnis et Chloé ".

1911

Cubism (BRAQUE, PICASSO, LÉGER, VILLON) at the Salon d'Automne.

1911-1913

The brothers PERRET build the Théâtre des Champs-Elysées.

1912

First performance of CLAUDEL's " L'Annonce faite à Marie " .

1913

Proust publishes " Du Côté de Chez Swann ".
First performance of STRAVINSKY's " Sacre du Printemps ".
Montparnasse and the " Paris School " (CHAGALL, MODIGLIANI, PASCIN, KISLING, SOUTINE).

1914

August 1st: Assassination of JAURÈS.
The Hôtel Biron ceded to RODIN by the State.

1919

Victory Parade down the Champs-Elysées. Interment of the Unknown Soldier beneath the Arc de Triomphe de l'Etoile.

1920

VALÉRY publishes " Le Cimetière Marin ".

1922

COCTEAU publishes " Thomas l'Imposteur ".

1923

First performance of " Knock " by Jules Romains.
RADIGUET publishes " Le Diable au Corps ".
Construction begins on the Cité Universitaire.

1924

Dadaism gives birth to Surrealism (ANDRÉ BRETON, PHILIPPE SOUPAULT).

1925

First Surrealist Exhibition (DE CHIRICO, ERNST, MIRO, KLEE, PICASSO, MAN RAY).

1928

First performance of HONNEGER's " Judith ".

1930-1932

LE CORBUSIER builds the Swiss Pavilion of the Cité Universitaire.

1931

Colonial Exposition.

1932

Assassination of President DOUMER.
MAURIAC publishes " Le Nœud de Vipères ".

1933

MALRAUX publishes " La Condition Humaine ".

1934

The February riots.

1935

First performance of " La Guerre de Troie n'aura pas Lieu " by GIRAUDOUX.

1937

Exposition of Arts and Techniques.
CARLU builds the Palais and the Théâtre de Chaillot.

1938

SARTRE publishes " La Nausée ".

1940

June 14: Occupation of Paris by the Germans.

1944

August 26: Liberation of Paris

PRINTED THE 30th OF SEPTEMBER 1956
THE HELIO-GRAVURE WAS PRINTED
BY BRAUN OF MULHOUSE AND THE
ILLUSTRATIONS IN COLOR
BY DRAEGER OF PARIS.